THE
KING'S
MISSION

A DAILY ADVENT DEVOTIONAL

J. AARON WHITE

CHRIST-
CENTERED
& CLEAR

To my wife,

partner in the gospel and fellow servant of the King.

CONTENTS

BORN TO LIVE

DECEMBER 1
THE ETERNAL SON

---

*Father, I desire that they also, whom you have given me, may be
with me where I am, to see my glory that you have given me
because you loved me before the foundation of the world.*

(John 17:24)

By now I am sure you have started humming classic Christmas songs (I bet some of you started secretly doing this months ago!). Assuredly one of the songs in your repertoire is the Isaac Watts classic, *Joy to the World*. Although the opening line is well-known, it is rarely plundered for its theological significance: "Joy to the world, the Lord is come!" Let's pause for a moment and ask an important question: *Where did he come from?*

Jesus himself helps us in our quest in what is known as his High Priestly Prayer (John 17). In that prayer, Jesus expresses his desire for his redeemed people to be with him in heaven for the primary reason of seeing his glory (Jn. 17:24). Immediately after his petition, he reveals that God the Father has loved him "before the foundation of the world." Other passages of Scripture also affirm the eternality of Jesus Christ:

"In the beginning was the Word, and the Word was with God, and the Word was God. He was in the beginning with God" (Jn. 1:1-2).

"Jesus said to them, 'Truly, truly, I say to you, before Abraham was, I am'" (Jn. 8:58).

It is impossible to fully grasp what it means to be with God, loved by God, and enjoyed by God, while being coequal with God from eternity past. The very notion of infinity is dizzying. Coupled with the mystery of the Trinity, we are forced to acknowledge our weakness and finitude as we bow in reverence and whisper, "Holy." When we sing, "Joy to the world, the Lord is come!" we are not declaring that he came into being when he arrived as a frail little baby in a manger stall—a thousand times no! Jesus Christ is not a created being nor is he a mere angel. He is exactly who Peter declared him to be: "You are the Christ, the Son of the living God" (Matt. 16:16). Consider the eternal love of the Trinity—Father, Son, and Holy Spirit—exploding like a million atom bombs in cascades of joy and adoration. Now, contrast that image with the words of Paul:

> Have this mind among yourselves, which is yours in Christ Jesus, who, though he was in the form of God, did not count equality a thing to be grasped, but made himself nothing, taking the form of a servant, being born in the likeness of men. And being found in human form, he humbled himself by becoming obedient to the point of death, even death on a cross (Phil. 2:5-8).

From the heights of glory to the depths of human frailty, the eternal Son of God came to earth. Fully God and fully man, the mystery of the Incarnation fills us with reverent awe. Moreover, when we consider that Jesus undertook this mission for unlovely, wrath-deserving rebels, we are further pressed into the dust of humility: "For while we were still weak, at the right time Christ died for the ungodly" (Rom. 5:6). The next time you hum *Joy to the World*, ponder the monolithic reality that the baby in Bethlehem antedates the universe by a billion millennia of joy-filled time. He is the eternal Son, the King.

DECEMBER 2
THE VIRGIN BIRTH

And the angel answered her, "The Holy Spirit will come upon you, and the power of the Most High will overshadow you; therefore the child to be born will be called holy—the Son of God."

(Luke 1:35)

Prepare to be offended: I do not like plastic Nativity scenes. There, I said it. Before you gasp in dismay and assume my dissent is theological in nature, let me assure you that I am being slightly facetious. Nevertheless, I do struggle with my own inclinations toward sentimentalism when it comes to gazing upon the warm glow of the holy family in someone's front yard. I often fail to grasp the richness of what that scene represents. Specifically, I fail to ponder the reality, magnitude, and significance of the virgin birth of my Lord and Savior.

How did it happen? The Bible clearly affirms that Mary was a virgin when she became pregnant with the Lord Jesus: "Now the birth of Jesus Christ took place in this way. When his mother Mary had been betrothed to Joseph, before they came together she was found to be with child from the Holy Spirit" (Matt. 1:18). Luke's account gives us a little more information on the matter: "And the angel answered [Mary], 'The Holy Spirit will come upon you, and the power of the Most High will overshadow you'" (Lk. 1:35). Scripture is unwavering in its declaration that Jesus had an earthly mother but no earthly father. Although modern science may bristle at such a seemingly nonsensical idea, the Word of God is clear, firm, and unyielding on this point of doctrine. As with spiritual rebirth (Jn. 3:5), Christ's physical birth was completely a sovereign work of God the Holy Spirit.

Why did it happen? There are numerous doctrinal implications connected to the virgin birth of Christ, each one worthy of concentrated study and relishing. His virgin birth ensured that he would truly be the God-man, what theologians refer to as the *hypostatic union* of Christ. Mary herself needed a Savior (Lk. 1:47); therefore, the Spirit protected the baby from original sin: "[Jesus] was tempted as we are, yet without sin" (Heb. 4:15). As a sinless man, Christ was able to offer himself as a sacrifice for sin since he himself was innocent and pure. The gospel would not be good news in any way if Jesus Christ were a sinner in the slightest measure. Only an impeccable man can declare that he always keeps the Father's commandments (Jn. 15:10). Only a sinless man could stand in the place of sinners as an acceptable sacrifice for their sins: "Christ also suffered once for sins, the righteous for the unrighteous, that he might bring us to God" (1 Pt. 3:18). It must be noted that he came "in the likeness of sinful flesh" (Rom. 8:3); he did not *become* sinful in himself.

His virgin birth not only ensured that "the child to be born [would] be called holy" (Lk. 1:35), it also ensured that he would be an effective Savior—Jesus lived the life of perfect obedience that his sinful people never could (Rom. 5:18-19). Moreover, his virgin birth ensured that he would be a sympathetic Savior. The author of Hebrews declares, "For we do not have a high priest who is unable to sympathize with our weaknesses, but one who in *every* respect has been tempted as we are, yet without sin" (Heb. 4:15, emphasis added). Famished with hunger? Jesus understands. Grieving a loss? Jesus understands. Weary from life's journey? Jesus understands. This is astounding.

When the light of a nativity scene (plastic or otherwise) illumines the frosty night air in your neighborhood, stop to ponder the significance of the virgin birth. Born without sin, being fully God and fully man, he was (and is) the perfect Savior. There is no one like him, Jesus Christ the Lord.

DECEMBER 3
THE LAW FULFILLED

But when the fullness of time had come, God sent forth his Son,
born of a woman, born under the law, to redeem those who were
under the law, so that we might receive adoption as sons.

(Galatians 4:4-5)

I often ask my children, "What did Jesus do for us?" With set jaws and puffed chests, they confidently reply, "He died for our sins!" True enough. However, it is always my delight to counter with another inquiry. With a raised eyebrow, I ask, "What else did Jesus do for us?" At this, my little flock begins to lose their conviction. At the height of the tense silence, I lower my voice and declare, "Jesus not only died for us, he lived for us too." There are fewer joys sweeter than explaining one of the most critical and astounding biblical doctrines to my wide-eyed children: *the active obedience of Christ.*

Paul wrote to the Galatian church to correct false teaching that was negatively impacting the congregations. Specifically, his apostolic fervor was aimed at reestablishing the sufficiency of Christ alone to save, not the law. Not only does Paul affirm the eternal existence of Christ (*God sent forth his Son*), he also affirms the full humanity of Christ (*born of woman*). Paul then makes another striking observation and declares that Christ was "born under the law, to redeem those who were under the law" (Gal. 4:4-5). Why was this necessary? Why couldn't Jesus have simply come to earth as a grown man and gone directly to the cross to pay for his people's sins?

Not only do we need our sins removed, we need a positive righteousness to be given to us! It would do us no good to simply have our sins removed and remain in a position of moral neutrality. Therefore Christ, as the Last Adam and representative of his people, lived in complete obedience to God's law—for us! This is what Paul was referring to when he said, "For as by the one man's disobedience the many were made sinners, so by the one man's obedience the many will be made righteous" (Rom. 5:19). Paul, himself an expert in the law, boldly exclaimed:

> Indeed, I count everything as loss because of the surpassing worth of knowing Christ Jesus my Lord. For his sake I have suffered the loss of all things and count them as rubbish, in order that I may gain Christ and be found in him, *not having a righteousness of my own that comes from the law, but that which comes through faith in Christ, the righteousness from God that depends on faith* (Phil. 3:8-9, emphasis added).

In his former life as a Pharisee, Paul assuredly knew and sought to obey the law (Phil. 3:5). However, once grace opened his eyes to the dual shock of his inner depravity and Christ's supreme holiness, he gladly disregarded his record of accomplishment in exchange for the perfect righteousness that Christ earned in his life of obedience. Paul canceled his ledger so that Christ's obedience could be credited to his account.

King Jesus not only came to die for his people, he came to live for them too. At his baptism, he declared his aim to "fulfill all righteousness" (Matt. 3:15). Though he was tempted throughout his life, he never violated God's law (Heb. 4:15). He alone can say, "I always do the things that are pleasing to him" (Jn. 8:29). It is because of his sinless life of perfect obedience that the great gospel summary can hold true: "For our sake he made him to be sin who knew no sin, so that in him we might become the righteousness of God" (2 Cor. 5:21). This Christmas, we not only celebrate the King who came to die for us, we rejoice in the King who came to live for us.

THE MESSIAH INDEED

For to us a child is born, to us a son is given; and the government shall be upon his shoulder, and his name shall be called Wonderful Counselor, Mighty God, Everlasting Father, Prince of Peace.

(Isaiah 9:6)

I t is difficult to separate the words of Isaiah's prophecy from the image of little boys wearing bath robes while holding wooden shepherd hooks. In thousands of churches, this scene has played out in innumerable Christmas pageants through the years (I myself donned a navy-blue bath robe whilst playing my role as a shepherd in 1986). Nevertheless, it is imperative that we rescue this monolithic proclamation from becoming too familiar in our minds and hearts. Failing to grasp the weight of this passage does great harm to the joy we would otherwise experience if we see it in context.

To mine the riches of Isaiah's prophecy, we must understand the word *Messiah*. In John's gospel, we see it used by Andrew: "He first found his own brother Simon and said to him, 'We have found the Messiah' (which means Christ)" (Jn. 1:41). In light of John's revelation, we must now define *Christ*. It derives from the Greek word *Christos* which means *anointed one*. In ancient Israel, God's chosen servants would be anointed with oil as a sign of being set apart: "Then Samuel took a flask of oil and poured it on [Saul's] head and kissed him and said, 'Has not the Lord anointed you to be prince over his people Israel?'" (1 Sam. 10:1). Although earthly kings and priests were anointed for God's service, it was the ultimate servant, the Messiah, whom the people of Israel longed for. Perhaps we can better understand the rancor that was stirred up in Jesus' hometown when he declared that Isaiah's prophecy concerning the anointed one was fulfilled in him (Isa. 61:1, Lk. 4:18-19). There is no doubt that Jesus Christ took upon himself the full weight of the Messianic title and expectations that permeate the entirety of the Old Testament.

Prophesying to the idolatrous people of Israel in the shadow of an imminent invasion by Assyria, Isaiah raises a banner of hope in chapter nine. In verse one, Isaiah declares that Galilee will be the sight of the Messiah's base of operations (Matt. 4:12-16). From there, Isaiah begins to describe what the coming Messiah (Christ) would be like and what his mission would entail. Unlike flawed human kings, the coming anointed one will bring light to those in (spiritual) darkness (Isa. 9:2). Moreover, the coming redeemer would arrive as a gift of God's magnificent grace—as a baby boy (Isa. 9:6). This child will rule the world in supreme power. He will be the ultimate king; he will be God. He will be the *Wonderful Counselor*, a ruler whose wisdom infinitely exceeds the shrewdness of Solomon. He will be the *Mighty God*, not a mere created being (Deut. 10:17). He will be the *Everlasting Father*, a king who cares for and shepherds his people with paternal care and tenderness (Jn. 10:14). He will be the *Prince of Peace*, the only ruler who can truly bring peace to earth through both mercy and judgment.

In case a molecule of doubt remains, let's consider the scene at the well in Samaria: "The woman said to him, 'I know that Messiah is coming (he who is called Christ). When he comes, he will tell us all things.' Jesus said to her, 'I who speak to you am he'" (Jn. 4:25-26). In this one statement, the full thrust of the Old Testament promises regarding the anointed one rush in. I had no idea what I was saying in 1986. May we, by God's grace, know, relish, and rejoice in what we are saying this year about the King.

DECEMBER 5
THE FINAL ADAM

And Jesus, full of the Holy Spirit, returned from the Jordan and was led by the Spirit in the wilderness for forty days, being tempted by the devil. And he ate nothing during those days. And when they ended, he was hungry.

(Luke 4:1-2)

If you or someone you know has served in the military, you have assuredly heard horror stories about the pains of group punishment. Picture a group of fresh, young recruits nervously standing at attention as the drill sergeant slowly inspects every bunk. You can almost hear every stomach churn as the stone-faced sergeant stops, gazes at a single wrinkle in bunk number seven, and shakes his head disapprovingly. The trembling recruit braces for his verdict. "Everybody on the floor! I want fifty push-ups right now!" screams the sergeant. Not only does the shamed owner of bunk seven start pushing, all of his comrades do too. This is the reality and genius of one member representing the whole.

With this in mind, let's leave the scene of our sweaty recruits and go further back in time, much further. Adam stands nervously before his maker. As the representative of humanity, we all stand unseen beside him. The verdict falls: "Because you have listened to the voice of your wife and have eaten of the tree of which I commanded you, 'You shall not eat of it,' cursed is the ground because of you" (Gen. 3:17). Our forefather's rebellion against his gracious Lord impacts all his progeny. This is what Paul refers to when he says, "For as in Adam all die" (1 Cor. 15:22). Adam did more than leave a wrinkle in his bunk. Our far-off grandfather

16

committed treason against the King of the universe. If redemption is to occur, a perfect representative will need to come and act on behalf of his people.

"But the free gift is not like the trespass. For if many died through one man's trespass, much more have the grace of God and the free gift by the grace of that one man Jesus Christ abounded for many" (Rom. 5:15). Could there be any sweeter words for the children of Adam? The Lord Jesus Christ, as the representative of his people, succeeded in every point where Adam failed. Jesus obeyed at every point that Adam rebelled. Adam was called to magnify God as his image bearer (Gen. 1:27) but only Jesus perfectly represented the Father (Jn. 14:9). Adam was called to worship and serve in the garden where he dwelled in God's presence (Gen. 2:15) but only Jesus was zealous for the purity of his Father's house (Ps. 69:9, Jn. 2:17). Adam was called to love and protect his bride (Gen. 2:24-25) but only Jesus perfectly loved and protected his bride (Eph. 5:25-27). Adam was called to protect the garden from unclean things but only Jesus refused to listen to the serpent. Adam gave ear to the hiss of the snake; Jesus gave him Scripture:

> And Jesus answered him, "It is said, 'You shall not put the Lord your God to the test.'" And when the devil had ended every temptation, he departed from him until an opportune time (Lk. 4:12-13).

Adam failed the test; Jesus passed with honors. The serpent snared the first representative but the One who represented all the elect shook the rope from his leg.

Like the red-faced recruits in the barracks, we all stand guilty (Rom. 3:23). The difference, however, is in the quality of the representatives. Adam was real as was his sin yet he was "a type of the one who was to come" (Rom. 5:14). The sad story of Adam is eclipsed by the power, might, and impeccable performance of Christ. This Christmas, we celebrate the superiority of the King, the last and superior Adam.

DECEMBER 6
THE SUPREME EXAMPLE

Have this mind among yourselves, which is yours in Christ Jesus.

(Philippians 2:5)

B e good for goodness' sake. Not only is this a line from a beloved Christmas tune, we've all heard this timeless adage spoken in one context or another. However, as any parent knows, it's power is limited at best. Soon after the phrase is uttered, the fighting in the back seat and the accusations of toy thievery resume. Oh well, so much for good intentions.

However, Jesus himself said, "If I then, your Lord and Teacher, have washed your feet, you also ought to wash one another's feet. For I have given you an example, that you also should do just as I have done to you" (Jn. 13:14-15). The apostle Peter calls upon Christ's example to encourage Christians to maintain humility in suffering: "For to this you have been called, because Christ also suffered for you, leaving you an example, so that you might follow in his steps" (1 Pet. 2:21). Is the essence of salvation simply following Christ's example of love and maintaining high moral standards? Certainly not! Salvation is a work of the Spirit of God in which he opens the eyes of the spiritually blind to see, savor, and follow Jesus Christ (2 Cor. 4:4-6). We are saved by grace alone through faith alone in Christ alone (Eph. 2:8-9). We are completely dependent on his grace to live the Christian life (Phil. 2:12-13); we are dependent on his grace to take our next breath (Acts 17:28). His death on the cross was a real sacrifice that satisfied the wrath of Almighty God on behalf of his people (Rom. 3:21-26). However, by the power of his grace, we are called, as Peter said, to follow in his steps. What example did King Jesus leave for his grace-dependent, Spirit-empowered people to follow?

He calls us to selfless humility. Paul exhorts the Philippian believers to adorn themselves with the attitude of Christ: "Have this mind among yourselves, which is yours in Christ Jesus" (Phil. 2:5). The great apostle already charged the Philippian believers to be united in their thinking (v. 2), joined in mutual love for one another (v. 2), seeking the honor of others instead of their own (v. 3), and seeking to minister to others and not simply their own needs (v. 4). After giving this lofty encouragement, Paul then exalts the ultimate model of such selfless humility, the Lord Jesus. As coeternal with the Father and full of regal majesty, Jesus set aside his kingly rights in order to be born as a baby who would fulfill the perfect law of God and die on a cross for the sins of his people. It is scandalous for the king of a small country to leave his throne to shine the shoes of his subjects. It is beyond the grasp of imagination that the rightful King of the universe would serve his sinful, rebellious people by washing their feet with water and washing their souls with his own blood. We cannot cleanse souls, but we can wash feet and fill bellies in the name of the King.

He calls us to patient endurance. Children know when justice must be served—to suffer unjustly or without cause is anathema! Nevertheless, God's people have always been marked by maltreatment in this world. It is into this exceedingly tough space that Peter says the unthinkable: suffer unjust treatment with patient endurance. Although our blood, unlike Christ's, does not cover sin, it nonetheless serves as a silent witness to our trust in God's sovereign justice (v. 23).

Being good for goodness' sake only leads to frustration and disenfranchisement. Following in the bloody footsteps of our King, trusting in his never-ending flow of grace, laying down our rights in selfless service, and patiently enduring suffering leads to his glory and our joy.

BORN TO DIE

DECEMBER 7
THE LAMB OF GOD

The next day he saw Jesus coming toward him, and said, 'Behold, the Lamb of God, who takes away the sin of the world!'"

(John 1:29)

Imagine this scene: A world-renowned dignitary walks into a crowded ball full of other high-class statesmen and people of power. The dignitary stands at the pinnacle of the stairs in a five-thousand-dollar suit with his beaming wife at his side. Both smile, awaiting the announcement of their much-anticipated arrival. A portly little man in a frumpy tuxedo swaggers to the center of the foyer and clears his throat, exclaiming, "Hey you guys, Bob and Cindy are here. They clean up pretty good, eh?" The very thought is cringe worthy. Regardless of training or conditioning, most people know when to show reverence for someone in a position of power. The uncouth, poorly dressed town crier missed his mark by a long shot!

Odd introductions are not foreign to Scripture. John the Baptist had a very fruitful ministry in calling sinners to repent and be baptized in preparation for the coming of the Messiah (Lk. 3:1-22). The people's Messianic curiosity was piqued:

As the people were in expectation, and all were questioning in their hearts concerning John [the Baptist], whether he might be the Christ, John answered them all, saying, "I baptize you with water, but he who is mightier than I is coming, the strap of whose sandals I am not worthy to untie. He will baptize you with the Holy Spirit and with fire. His winnowing fork is in his hand, to clear his threshing floor and to gather the wheat into his barn, but the chaff he will burn with unquenchable fire" (Lk. 3:15-17).

Knowing this makes John's announcement of Jesus even more perplexing. Considering John's words, one would expect a Messiah who baptizes in fire to ride into town with exceedingly great fanfare and trumpets bellowing the fearful tidings of his appearance. Not only did John fail to sound a trumpet blast, he cried out, "Behold, the *lamb* of God, who takes away the sin of the world!" (Jn. 1:29, emphasis added). Lamb? Wouldn't something like a bull, lion, or bear be more fitting for a fire-baptizing King?

Although seemingly odd, John's announcement was not inappropriate. In fact, it was perfect. Long before John stepped onto the religious scene of Israel, another prophet uttered these words: "He was oppressed, and he was afflicted, yet he opened not his mouth; like a lamb that is led to the slaughter, and like a sheep before its shearers is silent, so he opened not his mouth" (Isa. 53:7). The crowds were expecting the Messiah to vanquish their Roman oppressors and establish a kingdom that would match and exceed both David's and Solomon's. God's plan, however, was grander and more mysterious. His King would indeed dominate his foes—by way of his death on a cross and his rising from the grave (Col. 2:13-14). To Jewish ears, the word *lamb* would have evoked images of temple sacrifice, not kingship. To the ears of defiled sinners, however, it should evoke praise and adoration.

Peter gloried in the *lambness* of the King: "Knowing that you were ransomed from the futile ways inherited from your forefathers, not with perishable things such as silver or gold, but with the precious blood of Christ, like that of a lamb without blemish or spot" (1 Pet. 1:18-19). Jesus Christ is indeed the Lion of Judah whose roar causes his enemies to buckle in fear. He is also the Lamb of God who willingly offered his neck to the blade on behalf of his sinful people. This Christmas, may we stand in wide-eyed amazement at the announcement of the Lion-Lamb King.

DECEMBER 8

THE CURSE BEARER

Christ redeemed us from the curse of the law by becoming a curse for us—for it is written, "Cursed is everyone who is hanged on a tree."

(Galatians 3:13)

It's a classic plotline. The beautiful princess is cursed by a witch, the valiant prince overcomes savage adversity to rescue her, and the two live—well, you know the rest. In our day and age, the word *curse* is almost exclusively relegated to the realm of fairy tales (and filthy speech). In Scripture, however, it has much deeper and far-reaching implications. Infinitely more troublesome than a witch's incantation, being under the curse of Almighty God is the most devastating, severe, and dire of all circumstances. Sadly for us, this is exactly where our sin has placed us. Do we have a valiant prince willing to save us? Indeed, we do.

This Christmas, we celebrate the coming of the King who would undo what Adam wrought. Let's go back to Genesis to refresh our memories:

> The Lord God said to the serpent, "Because you have done this, *cursed* are you above all livestock" . . . And to Adam he said, "Because you have listened to the voice of your wife and have eaten of the tree of which I commanded you, 'You shall not eat of it,' *cursed* is the ground because of you" (Gen. 3:14, 17, emphasis added).

This is no mere curse given by a capricious magician. This is a formal legal edict pronounced upon sinful lawbreakers by the King and Sovereign of the universe! Adam, his children (the

24

human race), and even the earth itself lies under God's holy judgment (Jn. 3:36).

In his letter to the Galatian churches, Paul valiantly defends the gospel by reminding the troubled flock that seeking salvation by trying to keep the law is impossible: "For all who rely on works of the law are under a curse; for it is written, 'Cursed be everyone who does not abide by all things written in the Book of the Law, and do them'" (Gal. 3:10). Sinful humans cannot obey the law's demand of perfection—legal condemnation, a curse, is inevitable. James confirms this dire reality: "For whoever keeps the whole law but fails in one point has become accountable for all of it" (Jas. 2:10). What can be done to save the rebellious, criminally minded princess? It will require drastic, scandalous action.

Specifically, it will require that a ransom be paid out. In our story, it is the princess who is evil and needs to be bailed out. Amazingly, this is what the King does: "Christ redeemed us from the curse of the law by becoming a curse for us" (Gal. 3:13). The word *redeemed* (in Greek, *exagorazo*) refers to buying back a slave's freedom. How did the King buy his bride's freedom from sin's slavery? Paul reaches all the way back to the Book of Deuteronomy: "Cursed is everyone who is hanged on a tree" (Gal. 3:13, Deut. 21:23). In the Old Testament, an executed criminal was tied to a tree as a visible representation of being cut off from God by sin. Jesus Christ, the perfect Son of God, was hung on a tree (the cross) as the sinless substitute for his people. In short, Jesus bore the curse that they deserved: "He himself bore our sins in his body on the tree, that we might die to sin and live to righteousness. By his wounds you have been healed" (1 Pet. 2:24).

The thorns that were part of God's original curse (Gen. 3:18) were placed upon the head of the only person who could truly bear them. This Christmas, we stand in reverent awe of the King who became a curse for us.

THE GREAT EXCHANGE

For our sake he made him to be sin who knew no sin, so that in him we might become the righteousness of God.

(2 Corinthians 5:21)

There is always much talk of exchanging gifts this time of year. If your experience is anything like mine, you know that buying presents for other people can easily turn into a guilt-laden competition in which we press our budgets to breaking in order to secure a better gift than the other giver. If you get wind that your best friend is buying you a leather jacket, you rush out to get him a flat-screen television. The madness is unending. However, it would be exceedingly insulting to receive a leather jacket (or, in my case, a gift card to a book store and one hundred pounds of coffee) and give a dead racoon in exchange. An expensive coat for some roadkill is not a fair transaction. Nevertheless, this type of scandalous exchange is exactly what our King has done; theologians call it *the great exchange.*

In his second letter to the Corinthian church, Paul gives the gospel in a proverbial nutshell (2 Cor. 5:21). In this one verse, he cuts straight to the heart of the gospel. Therefore, it is worthy of sober unpacking:

For our sake—Humans have a nasty habit of thinking too highly of themselves. Therefore, it is good to ask who the "our" is in this verse. Did Jesus give his perfect life for nice, law-biding folks? No, Paul tells us elsewhere: "For we ourselves were once foolish, disobedient, led astray, slaves to various passions and pleasures, passing our days in malice and envy, hated by others and hating one another" (Titus 3:3). Bear this ugly picture in mind as we move further into 2 Corinthians 5:21.

He made him to be sin who knew no sin—The importance and mystery of this phrase cannot be overstated. Harkening back to our original analogy, Jesus got the roadkill—he took our sin. The King of the universe, worthy of being showered with gifts of pure gold and the finest oils was instead given the rotting filth of our transgressions. He did not *become* sin; he was *treated* as sin: "And the Lord has laid on him the iniquity of us all" (Isa. 53:6). As the substitute for his sinful people, Jesus bore the wrath that their sin deserved. Instead of wearing an expensive leather jacket, Jesus Christ willingly donned the tattered, bloody, putrid gown of his people's sin.

So that in him we might become the righteousness of God— The ones who gave the roadkill now receive the jacket. This is astounding. In fact, it would be more accurate to say that they receive a robe: "And the angel said to those who were standing before him, 'Remove the filthy garments from him.' And to him he said, 'Behold, I have taken your iniquity away from you, and I will clothe you with pure vestments'" (Zech. 3:4). Our soiled garments of sin are laid upon Christ while his sparkling garments of perfect righteousness are laid upon our undeserving shoulders. Just as God treats Christ as sinful, he now treats those who are united to him by faith as righteous (Rom. 1:17).

This year, as we exchange gifts with friends and loved ones, let us press beyond the clamber of consumerism and meditate upon the great exchange. We will spend a thousand ages of time in the presence of the Lamb in awestruck amazement that we are wearing the King's robes—to him be glory, honor, and praise!

DECEMBER 10
THE WRATH SATISFIER

Since, therefore, we have now been justified by his blood, much more shall we be saved by him from the wrath of God.

(Romans 5:9)

Why would someone want to think about God's wrath at Christmas? The holidays are supposed to be marked by nauseatingly happy songs, egg nog, twinkling lights, and nauseatingly happy songs (yes, I mentioned it twice). The Christmas story is about a cute little baby in a manger, traveling wise men, and angelic announcements, not wrath and fury. The answer to these satirical observations is simple: *no wrath, no gospel; no gospel, no joy.*

Just as we appreciate the dazzling display of stars in a pitch-black sky, so we also appreciate the brilliance of the arrival of the Savior-King as we understand the true nature of the sin he came to save us from. Paul tells us plainly that Christ saved us from the wrath of God (Rom. 5:9). To appreciate this striking declaration, we must understand the nature of God's wrath:

God's wrath is necessary—If I hate the idea of slaughtering innocent cows, out of necessity, I will hate hamburgers (for the record, I absolutely love hamburgers). Likewise, since God is holy and loves all that is pure, righteous, and in accord with his holy character, he must hate all that is opposed to his purity. In short, God is holy and just, attributes that necessitate his hatred of sin (Hab. 1:13).

God's wrath is intense—It is one thing for a limited, finite creature to be wrathful; it is another for an infinite, all-powerful

Creator to be incensed. We see God's wrath manifested in the Old Testament accounts of the flood and the annihilation of Sodom and Gomorrah. However, the New Testament also affirms the settled nature of God's wrath against sin: "Whoever believes in the Son has eternal life; whoever does not obey the Son shall not see life, *but the wrath of God remains on him*" (Jn. 3:36, emphasis added).

God's wrath is holy—May we never confuse God's holy disposition toward sin and rebellion with some kind of cosmic temper tantrum! God is perfect in his attributes; he does not have to choose between being holy or wrathful. This may be difficult to imagine since our human anger is never pure and wholly righteous. God, however, is purely holy in all he does and in all that he is—including his wrath.

God's wrath is praiseworthy—Scripture never apologizes or blushes when speaking of God's wrath and neither should we. This is because it is a good thing that God hates sin. If he did not hate sin and either ignored or tolerated it, he would cease being holy! In the final analysis, God's wrath against sin will ultimately be praised: "Hallelujah! Salvation and glory and power belong to our God, for his judgments are true and just" (Rev. 19:1-2).

With all of these things in mind, we ought to marvel that God saved us from his wrath by pouring it on the head of his beloved Son (1 Jn. 4:10). Jesus' death on the cross was a wrath-satisfying sacrifice—he stood between his sinful people and the atomic blast furnace of God's righteous fury. Sin deserves nothing less than God's unmitigated wrath. This is exactly what Christ endured on the cross as our wrath-bearing King. When we understand God's wrath, we begin to understand the gospel; as we dive deeper into the gospel, our joy in our King increases.

DECEMBER 11
THE RANSOM PAID

Worthy are you to take the scroll and to open its seals, for you were slain, and by your blood you ransomed people for God.

(Revelation 5:9a)

The word *ransom* inspires intrigue. Thoughts of kidnapping, espionage, cryptic ransom letters, and getaway cars usually pop into our media-saturated minds when we hear this word. Whether it is a Hollywood film about a kidnapped senator or a novel about a captured princess, the notion of ransom points to the fact that someone is trapped, imprisoned, stuck, and helpless. The person in question cannot save themselves and is completely dependent on outside help. Specifically, they need someone to pay for their freedom, to secure their release from bondage.

One of the reasons we rejoice over the arrival of our Savior-King is that he came to redeem his enslaved people. Although we do not like to see ourselves as slaves, that is precisely the reality that Scripture points to: "you who were once *slaves of sin*" (Rom. 6:17, emphasis added). The writer of Hebrews says that Christ came to "deliver all those who through fear of death were subject to lifelong slavery" (Heb. 2:15). If we stop and analyze the lyrics of many of the old, beloved Christmas tunes, we find that redemption from sin factors into many of them. To look at it from yet another angle, the fact that we are singing about the coming Redeemer is a tacit affirmation that we are indeed in need of saving, in need of being ransomed.

Returning to our opening analogy, when the bad guys in a crime drama kidnap someone, the ransom must be paid to them to secure the victim's release. The question in regard to Scripture is, "To whom did Jesus pay our ransom?" This is a loaded question indeed! The seemingly logical answer would be that, since we are enslaved to sin and Satan, the ransom must have been paid to the devil. This idea was espoused by the early church theologian Origin and is categorically incorrect. The reason for rejecting this notion is twofold: Scripture nowhere teaches it and God is the offended party, not Satan. Not only will you not find a passage of Scripture that describes Christ's death as a payment made to the devil to secure our release, the very notion flies in the face of the nature of Christ's atoning death. Jesus died to satisfy *God's* holy law, not Satan's. However, we must also acknowledge that God was not holding us as captives, we were sin-loving slaves of the "prince of the power of the air" (Eph. 2:2). Without pressing the analogy too far, we simply affirm that we broke God's law, were captive to sin and Satan, and needed to be redeemed.

The jaw-dropping reality that the eternal Son of God humbly came to ransom his sinful, law-breaking bride from the bonds of sin makes even the greatest Hollywood thriller look like a black-and-white silent film. In the movies, the kidnapping victim is (usually) portrayed as innocent, wholesome, and altogether worthy of paying the full amount of the ransom demanded. In the case of the ones that Christ came to redeem, it is not so. The bride that Jesus came to save was like Hosea's wife: "And the Lord said to me, 'Go again, love a woman who is loved by another man and is an adulteress, even as the Lord loves the children of Israel, though they turn to other gods and love cakes of raisins'" (Hos. 3:1).

The sinless King gave his life to ransom his wandering bride, a spouse who willingly traded the joy of his glory for cakes of raisins. The mystery and majesty of Christmas is found in the pursuing love of the King: "Husbands, love your wives, as Christ loved the church and gave himself up for her" (Eph. 5:25).

THE VINDICATION OF GOD

It was to show his righteousness at the present time, so that he might be just and the justifier of the one who has faith in Jesus.

(Romans 3:26)

The gospel is primarily about God, not us. This realization is both devastating to our fragile egos and soul-satisfyingly liberating. At a time of year when we are tempted to focus on ourselves (i.e. our family, our gifts, our traditions, our agenda), it is good medicine to be confronted with the reality that "from him and through him and to him are all things" (Rom. 11:36). It is no less true regarding the good news of the gospel. The apostle Paul aptly refers to it as "the gospel of God" (Rom. 1:1). Although we obviously factor into the gospel as the recipients of abounding grace and mercy, the witness of Scripture does not place us at the epicenter of God's design in the cross. The cross is primarily about God.

Need more convincing? Let's go back and revisit one of the biggest tabloid scandals of the Old Testament: David's sin with Bathsheba. After being blessed in abundant measure by God, David dwells in opulence as the king of Israel. In a disgusting act of defiance and selfishness, David commits adultery with the wife of one of his most loyal soldiers (2 Sam. 11:1-5). After learning that she was pregnant with his child, David compounded his sin by arranging the murder of her husband (2 Sam. 11:14-27). In the estimation of most people, David is a scoundrel and worthy of severe punishment. Yet, David is listed in Hebrews chapter eleven as one of the faithful saints who was loved by God (Heb. 11:32). How can a holy God permit a worm like David to enter heaven?

The tension regarding David's sin and subsequent salvation is at the heart of Paul's reasoning in the closing verses of Romans chapter three, a section that many theologians consider to be the heart of the gospel. Paul summarizes his argument about humanity's sinfulness and guilt (Rom. 3:23) then focuses on the primary motivation of God putting his beloved Son on the cross: "This was to show God's righteousness, because in his divine forbearance he had passed over former sins" (Rom. 3:25). Did you catch that? The sinless death of Jesus Christ on the cross served a *displaying* function. Namely, it displayed God's righteousness. Paul gives his own commentary by explaining that such a display was necessary since God had "passed over former sins." In other words, David was not punished with the full weight of God's wrath since God was looking forward to the cross where David's sins would be paid for. If anyone throughout the Old Testament period was wondering if God, the righteous judge of the universe, was sweeping the sins of his people under some cosmic rug, the cross silences all such grumbling and accusation.

Paul repeats and explains himself since this is such a crucial issue: "[The cross] was to show his righteousness at the present time, so that he might be just and the justifier of the one who has faith in Jesus" (Rom. 3:26). How can Almighty God forgive and befriend men such as David, Moses, Abraham, and countless other Old Testament saints—all of whom were sinners through and through? What prevents Satan, the accuser, from pointing his crooked finger in God's direction and crying, "Unjust!"? Paul tells us the answer: *the cross of Jesus Christ.*

The cross vindicates God's holiness by holding up his bloody sacrificial Lamb whose sinless substitution for his people forever silences all doubts regarding God's holiness. The gospel of God upholds the holiness of God by exalting the Son of God as the Lamb of God. Christ satisfied justice. It is the joy of all David-like sinners to see the cross of Christ lifted high since we know that our joy is found in making much of him, not ourselves.

BORN TO RISE

DECEMBER 13
THE HOPE OF BELIEVERS

If the Spirit of him who raised Jesus from the dead dwells in you,
he who raised Christ Jesus from the dead will also give life to
your mortal bodies through his Spirit who dwells in you.

(Romans 8:11)

Ours would be a lackluster celebration if the King remained dead. His legacy would be reduced to a bronze statue in a city square while his tired bones gathered dust in a sepulcher somewhere. This is the fate of even the mightiest of human authorities. Statues, busts, paintings, ornate headstones, and plaques are kind overtures to remember their earthly conquests but the fact remains: death had the final word. If Jesus, like all other kings and dignitaries, succumb to the undertow of death, there would not be much to rejoice over. If he was simply a good moral teacher, our joy would be reduced to appreciation; our exuberance would be dulled to sentimental fondness. We would have great insights into compassion and love, but no real hope for our own dance with death.

The hope that we exult in this time of year (and every day) hinges on the historical reality of the resurrection of King Jesus. Unlike every other human ruler whose legacy ended in the grave, Jesus' eternal kingship was confirmed by his victory over death. The New Testament abounds with evidence of this momentous event:

> For I delivered to you as of first importance what I also received: that Christ died for our sins in accordance with the Scriptures, that he was buried, that he was raised on the third

day in accordance with Scriptures, and that he appeared to Cephas, then to the twelve. Then he appeared to more than five hundred brothers at one time, most of whom are still alive, though some have fallen asleep (1 Cor. 15:3-6).

Paul was keenly aware of the significance of Christ's resurrection from the dead. In fact, he banked the entirety of our faith and eternal destiny on it: "And if Christ has not been raised, your faith is futile and you are still in your sins" (1 Cor. 15:17). Paul's point is devastatingly simple: no resurrection, no hope.

Let's be clear—the hope of Christians is not only legal pardon before God (2 Cor. 5:21), it is also physical resurrection in glorified bodies like our Lord. This is what Paul alludes to when he says, "For in this tent we groan, longing to put on our heavenly dwelling" (2 Cor. 5:2). The aged apostle John also assures us that when our King returns in glory, we will obtain glorified bodies like the one he possesses: "Beloved, we are God's children now, and what we will be has not yet appeared; but we know that when he appears we shall be like him, because we shall see him as he is" (1 Jn. 3:2). The Holy Spirit that now indwells all of God's adopted children is a kind of down payment, a surety of what is to come: "If the Spirit of him who raised Jesus from the dead dwells in you, he . . . will also give life to your mortal bodies" (Rom. 8:11). For believers who love the Lord but groan under the weight of minds and bodies that are still susceptible to sin, disease, temptation, and death, the sure hope of our own resurrection is a precious and fragrant balm.

As we place gifts inside bags and packages this year, perhaps our minds will seize upon the analogy. Maybe we will think about the precious gift of the indwelling Spirit wrapped inside our frail flesh, a gift of immense grace that testifies to our future hope of resurrection. The same Spirit who was powerfully present at our Lord's own resurrection now dwells in us—this is worth a lifetime of joyful pondering. Our King not only came to die for our sins, he came to conquer death. If your Christmas is bathed in tears and grief, look to the risen Christ, and find hope of eternal life.

DECEMBER 14
THE SURETY OF SALVATION

Blessed be the God and Father of our Lord Jesus Christ! According to his great mercy, he has caused us to be born again to a living hope through the resurrection of Jesus Christ from the dead.

(1 Peter 1:3).

At the risk of reinforcing a view of Christmas that many believers try to downplay, I enjoy watching my kids open presents that their mother and I got them. Granted, we must be vigilant in our war against the gravitational pull of consumerism. However, I get joy from watching my little ones open a gift that I have been hiding in a top-secret location (my closet) for months. Nevertheless, these sweet moments can easily be tarnished. Imagine if I said, "You know, all of this is only possible because your mom and I spent our money on you." Although true, it seems awkward and inappropriate to discuss the source of blessing amidst the exuberance of giving and receiving.

In typical Peter-esque fashion, the bold apostle violates this rule of gift-giving and gushes over the source of our joy. The burly fisherman is not a bit reserved about the reason believers should be joyful. First, he gives credit where it is ultimately due: "Blessed be the God and father of our Lord Jesus Christ! According to his great mercy, he has caused us to be born again to a living hope" (1 Pet. 1:3). If we know ourselves to be born again, saved, regenerated, etc., it is owing *exclusively* to God who shows mercy. The gift of salvation comes from the hand of a gracious, merciful, loving, and holy God who sent his beloved Son to die as a ransom to redeem hell-deserving sinners. We did nothing to merit such a great salvation; we did nothing to effect our rebirth. God the Holy Spirit "caused us to be born again." Even our faith was and is a gift of grace: "For by grace you have been saved through faith. And this is not your own doing; it [including faith] is the gift of God, not a result of works, so that no one may boast" (Eph. 2:8-9). Peter knows that our joy will be *increased* by pointing to the source of our blessing. When it comes to salvation, the normal rules for gift-giving simply don't apply.

Secondly, Peter goes on to explain that the gift of salvation is explicitly linked to the resurrection of Jesus Christ: ". . . through the resurrection of Jesus Christ from the dead" (1 Pet. 1:3). Although our bodies are not yet glorified as was Christ's, we nevertheless enjoy new spiritual life and the hope of future glory because of his rising in power from the grave. Peter unashamedly tells us that our salvation was secured by Christ's victory over death. What a glorious play on words: since we have a *living* Savior and King, we have a "living hope." Dead kings cannot give living hope. Living, reigning, ruling, loving, thinking, speaking, sovereign, eternal kings can—and there is only One. When God raised Christ from the grave, he thought of us (his people) as rising with him: "But God, being rich in mercy, because of the great love with which he loved us, even when we were dead in our trespasses, *made us alive together with Christ*—by grace you have been saved" (Eph. 2:4-5, emphasis added). By our union with the risen Christ, we are raised to new spiritual life now and will one day be raised in glorified bodies.

Although it may be distasteful to tell the one you give a gift to how many hours of overtime you put in to afford it, knowing and understanding the surety of the gift of salvation increases our joy instead of diminishing it. Peter does us a great service by telling us exactly how we came to taste and see the grace of God. As we rejoice in our great salvation, we are directed to the empty tomb and the occupied throne as glorious reminders of how we came to be born again to a living hope!

DECEMBER 15
THE POWER TO LIVE

We were buried therefore with him by baptism into death, in order
that, just as Christ was raised from the dead by the glory of
the Father, we too might walk in newness of life.

(Romans 6:4)

I love December; I hate January. The merriment and anticipation of the holidays come to a grinding halt on January 1 around lunch time. As I sit at my kitchen table, somberly chewing a turkey and cheese sandwich, I look out of my window and see a Siberian wasteland of leafless trees and merciless snow drifts (let all those who live in the upper Midwest understand). The back yard where I would smilingly mow the grass and play soccer in the life-giving sunshine turns into a scene from a dystopian novel in which nuclear fallout has brought on an eternal winter. However, as spring slowly breaks winter's icy hold, an annual miracle manifests itself in silent power. Life begins to burst forth in the form of fresh buds, sprigs of green grass, and chirping birds. I am always amazed at the contrast between the deadness of January and the vivacious colors and sounds of May.

The shift from winter to spring is a parable of the Christian life. The apostle Paul sets forth this contrast in his letter to the Ephesians:

And you were dead in the trespasses and sins in which you once walked, following the course of this world, following the prince of the power of the air, the spirit that is now at work in the sons of disobedience—among whom we all once lived in the passions of our flesh, carrying out the desires of the body and the mind, and were by nature children of wrath, like the rest of mankind. But God, being rich in mercy, because of the great love with which he loved us, even when we were dead in our trespasses, made us alive together with Christ—by grace you have been saved (Eph. 2:1-5).

Due to our sinful nature, all of mankind exists in the realm of spiritual death. We are like zombies—dead but walking. Paul told us that we willingly followed our sinful desires but were dead and unresponsive to God's glory. The greatest need of any human being at any given moment is to be made spiritually alive by God.

This is exactly what happens in regeneration: God causes us to be spiritually alive. It is all of grace. In Romans chapter six, Paul likens our baptism in water to the salvation experience. Just as the person being baptized is immersed in water, Christ was lowered into the grave. Likewise, just as Christ was raised in power from the grave, the baptized person is raised from the water. By our union with Christ, his death and resurrection become ours! Not only is this good news for the future Day of Judgment, it is good news for our daily existence since we now "walk in newness of life." Just as our Lord received new life in his resurrection, we too have a new life. A new flavor marks the believer: salty. To be precise, the fruit of righteousness begins to season our thoughts, words, and actions. Although not completely free from sin's indwelling power, believers are nonetheless raised to a new life, a life of loving righteousness and pursuing joy in Christ.

Just like the lifeless trees in my backyard, sinners are leafless and cold. But just as Christ was raised to new life, the Spirit of God grants life where there is only death, taste where there is only blandness, and sight where there is only blindness. In union with our risen and living Lord, we walk in newness of life. The buds of love, joy, peace, patience, kindness, goodness, faithfulness, gentleness, and self-control begin to sprout on our branches. The trees wave their leafy branches in praise to the sovereign King who brought it about—we should do the same.

DECEMBER 16
THE SOURCE OF JUSTIFICATION

Who was delivered up for our trespasses and
raised for our justification.

(Romans 4:25)

P ermit me to make an unseasonal analogy. A man donning an orange jumpsuit and handcuffs is escorted into the silent courtroom. His grim face betrays a sense of internal dread. The judge sits high up on his bench like an eagle perched, ready to pounce upon a tiny field mouse. As the doomed criminal takes his place before the judge, a file is handed up to the black-robed official. The judge opens the file and reads aloud, "Mr. Badguy McNotsonice, the evidence against you is clear and airtight. You have murdered five innocent people, robbed three banks at gunpoint, burned down a public library, and cut the warning label off no less than eight mattresses." The judge then says something utterly unforeseen, "However, since I am a loving judge, I am going to let you go free." The courtroom gasps in disbelief. Then, one by one, they begin to chant with furor, "Fire the judge! Fire the judge!" The audience knows that, in the case of McNotsonice, justice has *not* been served.

Although ridiculous, this scenario primes our minds for the shocking and glorious doctrine of justification by faith alone. Simply defined, justification is an instant act of God in which he legally declares us to be righteous. We, like the criminal (I will spare you from reading his name again), stand completely guilty before the holy Judge of the universe. However, we have something that you-know-who didn't have: the perfect defense attorney. The apostle Paul tells us that we are pardoned and at peace with God: "Therefore, since we have been justified by faith, we have peace with God through our Lord Jesus Christ" (Rom. 5:1). Earlier in the Book of Romans, Paul explained how God's holiness could be maintained even though he pardons guilty sinners: "[The cross of Christ] was to show his righteousness at the present time, so that he might be just and the justifier of the one who has faith in Jesus" (Rom. 3:26). The cross stands as the ultimate proof that divine justice has been served regarding our sins: Jesus Christ shed his innocent blood for them. On this basis alone are sinners justified in God's sight.

Standing in a courtroom is daunting. Standing before the blazing eyes of Almighty God is unimaginable. How do we know that God accepted Christ's sacrifice for our sins? If Jesus simply died on the cross and remained in the tomb, we would have very little hope that his atonement for sin was effective. In light of our dire situation, Paul's words at the end of Romans chapter four are precious: "[Jesus] was delivered up for our trespasses and raised for our justification" (Rom. 4:25). We have absolute certainty that his sacrifice on our behalf was fully accepted by God because he rose from the dead! As often as we rejoice in our great salvation, we ought also to rejoice in the resurrection of Christ.

Sadly, there are some who only feel compelled to enter a church building on two occasions annually: Christmas and Easter. Nevertheless, if presented rightly, these dear souls may receive clear teaching about two of the greatest truths in Scripture, truths that are intimately connected: King Jesus came and died for sin; King Jesus defeated death and rose from the grave for our justification. The great apostle Paul would compel us to not wait until Easter to rejoice over the resurrection of our King. As we rejoice over his coming to deal with our sin on the cross, may we also glory in the fact that God fully accepted his sacrifice. The empty tomb bears witness to the scandal of our justification.

THE REASON TO RUN

*That by any means possible I may attain
the resurrection from the dead.*

(Philippians 3:11)

I saw it sitting there and my heart leapt in my chest. Although my dear mother tried to conceal its shape with excess packaging, I knew a plastic B-52 bomber when I saw one. Not only was it nearly three feet in length, it contained a payload of one hundred plastic soldiers and an envoy jeep inside its massive belly. My excitement was soon tempered as, with dread, I realized that it was only December fourth! Day after agonizing day I walked past the bulky red and white gift, tempting me with the allurement of endless joy and military conquest. I could almost hear her propellers thundering through the air as my mother would enter the room. I dared not let on that I knew what the gift was since she always threatened to take away my present if I guessed what they were (I realize now that she was kidding but it worked at the time). My insatiable craving for that plastic plane carried me through the last painful days of school until Christmas break. Finally, the big day arrived. Usually one's reality rarely meets expectations when anticipation is so high—but not with my B-52 bomber. It met and exceeded all expectations. I flew well over two hundred successful bombing raids in that plane without leaving the quiet confines of my backyard.

Infinitely more important than a bombing run, the apostle Paul was exceedingly motivated to run the race of faith until the end. In fact, he described his efforts this way: "Forgetting what lies behind and straining forward to what lies ahead, I press on toward the goal for the prize of the upward call of God in Christ Jesus" (Phil. 3:13-14). Like a marathon runner with bulging leg muscles, Paul likened his earthly pilgrimage to one of striding with sweat and fervor toward the finish line of heaven. He had already expressed his desire to see his Lord: "I am hard pressed between the two. My desire is to depart and be with Christ, for that is far better. But to remain in the flesh is more necessary on your account" (Phil. 1:23-24). Paul longed for the day that he would see Jesus face-to-face in glory. He did not find a nice shade tree to sit under and nap until his life expired (or a plush golf course for that matter). No, he ran with all his might while keeping a single-eyed devotion on the goal of Christlikeness in this life and Christ's presence in the next.

How can a sinner like Paul (or us) run with the hope of attaining some measure of Christlikeness in this life? Paul tells lets us in on a vital truth: "That I may know him and the power of his resurrection, and may share in his sufferings, becoming like him in his death" (Phil. 3:10). Like his Lord, Paul was willing to go to the limits to bring the good news of the gospel to sinners. In doing so, he suffered greatly (e.g. shipwreck, beatings, hunger, anxiety, persecution). In his sufferings, he found a deep and intimate fellowship with Christ. The power that raised Jesus from the grave was powerfully felt by Paul in his moments of gospel-centered suffering. Moreover, Paul had a hope that fueled his running: "That by any means possible I may attain the resurrection from the dead" (Phil. 3:11). Not only did he long for intimate fellowship with the risen Christ in this life, he looked forward to the sure hope that as Christ was physically raised to life, he would be also. Resurrection consumed Paul's thoughts.

I endured long hours of daydreaming in school as I waited to unveil my beloved bomber. Paul endured long days and nights of physical torture, fear, hunger, anxiousness, and loneliness by being embraced by his beloved King. More than a plastic plane, this King promises that just as he lives in a glorified body, so shall his sweaty marathoners. Run to the King!

DECEMBER 18
THE JOY OF UNION

Blessed be the God and Father of our Lord Jesus Christ,
who has blessed us in Christ with every spiritual
blessing in the heavenly places.

(Ephesians 1:3)

What's yours is mine and what's mine is ours. What a lovely though rarely realized overture of affection. If I receive a brand-new car for Christmas, I would likely refer to it as "my car" in accord with my innately selfish nature (though my beautiful wife would quickly correct me). Be honest for a moment. If you received an extraordinarily expensive gift (e.g. new car, private jet, space shuttle), would your first thought be to label it a *community* gift? Unless you are unusually sanctified, my guess is no.

With Christ, it is a different story. He is a King unlike any other king. He not only possesses the greatest strength, he possesses the greatest riches in the universe. Some kings command armies of thousands. King Jesus commands kings. Some kings order hundreds of servants to do their bidding. King Jesus orders entire solar systems to function as they do. There is simply no comparison. This is what makes the doctrine of our union with Christ so utterly astounding.

The New Testament writers point to the idea of our union with Christ by using the little preposition *in Christ* over one hundred times. "Therefore, if anyone is *in Christ*, he is a new creation. The old has passed away; behold, the new has come" (2 Cor. 5:17, emphasis added). "There is therefore now no condemnation for those who are *in Christ Jesus*" (Rom. 8:1, emphasis added). Not only does Scripture say that, by faith, we are in Christ, it also affirms the amazing reality that he is in us. Paul boldly declared, "I have been crucified with Christ. It is no longer I who live, but Christ who lives in me. And the life I now live in the flesh I live by faith in the Son of God, who loved me and gave himself for me" (Gal. 2:20). The seasoned apostle John made a similar assertion: "By this we know that we abide in him and he in us, because he has given us his Spirit" (1 Jn. 4:13). Like a branch on a vine, we are intimately connected (see John 15).

By being joined to Christ by faith, believers become co-heirs with their King. The risen King, the rightful heir of every blessing and honor, shares his bounty with his family: "And if children, then heirs—heirs of God and fellow heirs with Christ, provided we suffer with him in order that we may also be glorified with him" (Rom. 8:17). Paul told the Ephesians that, in Christ, we are blessed with "every spiritual blessing in the heavenly places." What does this blessing entail? What are the riches we receive by being joined to King Jesus?

We receive a new family - "For you did not receive a spirit of slavery to fall back into fear, but you have received the Spirit of adoption as sons, by whom we cry, 'Abba! Father!'" (Rom. 8:15).

We receive a new hope - "So that being justified by his grace we might become heirs according to the hope of eternal life" (Titus 3:7).

We receive a new honor - "The one who conquers, I will grant him to sit with me on my throne, as I also conquered and sat down with my Father on his throne" (Rev. 3:21).

None of these blessings would flow to branches through a dead vine. We do not gain an inheritance because our husband-King died. We are blessed because our living King gladly shares the spoils of his victory with his beloved. Every utterance of thanks this Christmas can be linked to union with Christ.

BORN TO REIGN

DECEMBER 19
THE ONLY TRUE KING

And Jesus came and said to them, "All authority in heaven and on earth has been given to me."

(Matthew 28:18)

I can think of at least two popular films that are based on the same basic plotline: the good king is usurped by an evil brother and is forced to regain his throne. As you probably guessed, swords are drawn and sides are taken as the beloved king rallies his loyal forces against the hordes of rebels who blindly support the nasty other brother. At the height of the battle, the good king and bad king meet atop the castle. With thrilling sword play, well-timed theme music, and breathtaking close calls, the good king eventually vanquishes his foe. The scene fades as the music takes on a major key. Crowds gather and cheer as the good king reclaims his throne. We're all suckers for this kind of storyline but I doubt that we would want to live in such a volatile kingdom. Thankfully, there is a King whose reign is uncontested, immovable, and eternal.

After rising from the dead and appearing to many, Jesus gathers his troops for a final muster in which they will be commissioned, charged, and deployed. Before sending them into battle, he grounds his orders on his prerogative to be able to command their loyalty: "And Jesus came and said to them, 'All authority in heaven and on earth has been given to me'" (Matt. 28:18). It is a great incentive to serve a general who has the full authority of the United States' military. It is an unspeakable privilege and rock-solid incentive to serve a general who possesses *all* authority—absolute sovereign authority. Over what does King Jesus hold sovereign sway?

Stars and Planets—"Long ago, at many times and in many ways, God spoke to our fathers by the prophets, but in these last days he has spoken to us by his Son, whom he appointed the heir of all things, *through whom also he created the world.* He is the radiance of the glory of God and the exact imprint of his nature, and *he upholds the universe by the word of his power*" (Heb. 1:1-3, emphasis added).

Spiritual and physical rulers—"He is the image of the invisible God, the firstborn of all creation. For by him all things were created, in heaven and on earth, visible and invisible, whether thrones or dominions or rulers or powers or authorities—all things were created through him and for him" (Col. 1:15-16).

The cross and the grave—"This Jesus, delivered up according to the definite plan and foreknowledge of God, you crucified and killed by the hands of lawless men. God raised him up, loosing the pangs of death, because it was not possible for him to be held by it" (Acts 2:23-24).

The well-being of his troops—"Now to him who is able to keep you from stumbling and to present you blameless before the presence of his glory with great joy, to the only God, our Savior, through Jesus Christ our Lord, be glory, majesty, dominion, and authority, before all time and now and forever. Amen" (Jude 24-25).

There is only one King whose rule and authority are absolute, sovereign, and unending. Earthly kings are frail and transient, never able to guarantee the ultimate good of their devotees. This Christmas, we do not rejoice in a beloved but mortal earthly power. We are glad to lay down our lives in the service of King Jesus since we know that *nothing* can stop him.

DECEMBER 20
THE SEATED PRIEST

And every priest stands daily at his service, offering repeatedly the same sacrifices, which can never take away sins. But when Christ had offered for all time a single sacrifice for sins, he sat down at the right hand of God, waiting from that time until his enemies should be made a footstool for his feet.

(Hebrews 10:11-14)

You can always tell when folks are getting anxious about the holidays. With food to prepare, gifts to buy, schedules to juggle, calls to make, letters to write, and homes to clean, we are often frantic, distracted, and unmerry merrymakers. We may not literally wring our hands in worry but we certainly betray a sense of being out of control with our frenzied busyness. If there were any doubt that we are not sovereign but are limited in our abilities, the holidays often serve as an annual dose of humility. We may want to be Mary, but our actions make us Martha.

What a contrast exists between our pathetic rushing and Christ's current position in heaven. We are busy, worried, anxious, and stressed. He is none of these; he is seated. Anxious people don't sit down. Worried people pace the floor. Those with tasks unfinished recoil at the idea of taking a seat. What then is the significance of King Jesus, our Great High Priest, and his current position of sitting? Why is it a good thing to serve a seated Priestly King? At a time of year when frenzy permeates the air, it is refreshing and encouraging to cast our eyes to the One whose work is complete and whose heart is at ease. Let's walk through this glorious section of the Book of Hebrews together:

Earthly priests always stand—The Old Testament Levitical system had hundreds of priests who were tasked with attending to the daily worship of Israel. These men were consecrated to offer sacrifices to Yahweh on behalf of the people: "And you shall say to them, This is the food offering that you shall offer to the Lord: two male lambs a year old without blemish, day by day, as a regular offering" (Num. 28:3). These earthly priests were always busy "offering repeatedly the same sacrifices, which can never take away sins" (Heb. 10:11). All the tireless efforts of all the priests over all the years were not enough to settle the issue of human sin.

Christ is the seated Great High Priest—Unlike the myriad earthly priests (sinners themselves who offered imperfect animals), Jesus was able to effectively deal with sin by his own sacrifice. Isaiah prophesied about the coming King who would provide the perfect lamb to atone for sin—himself: "He was oppressed, and he was afflicted, yet he opened not his mouth; like a lamb that is led to the slaughter, and like a sheep that before its shearers is silent, so he opened not his mouth" (Isa. 53:7). Drawing from Psalm 110, the author of Hebrews tells us that after making a full and effective atonement for sin, Jesus "sat down at the right hand of God" (Heb. 10:12, see Ps. 110:1). Jesus, the supreme Priest-King, is not hurriedly running around the heavenly temple. He is seated in regal majesty, a silent declaration that his work is finished.

The Old Testament sacrifices could not effectively deal with sin and could not close the mouth of the accuser, Satan. Through the cross, however, King Jesus dealt a death blow to the old serpent and his evil hordes (Col. 2:14-15, Heb. 2:14). He certainly intercedes for his elect even now, those who are "being sanctified" (Heb. 10:14, Rom. 8:31-34). However, his sovereign rule is firmly established. Although we may be frantic, our Great High Priest-King is firmly settled on his throne.

DECEMBER 21
THE HEAD OF THE CHURCH

And he is the head of the body, the church. He is the beginning, the firstborn from the dead, that in everything he might be preeminent.

(Colossians 1:18)

Let's go, we're going to be late!" the man yelled as he descended the creaky stairs while simultaneously tying an uneven knot in his only necktie. Three kids under the age of ten and one frazzled wife in a slightly wrinkled red blouse march down the stairs and into their trusty but frigid family van. The ride to church that evening was bittersweet—sweet because it was a yearly tradition yet bitter because it always produced anxiety. Arriving in the crowded parking lot of the state-of-the-art church facility at 6:58pm, the family scrambled out of the van that was just starting to warm up. Once inside, the roar of voices filled the crowded lobby as the father forced a smile to his face as he led his brood through the sea of people and into a vacant pew near the back. The man took in the spectacle of lights, cameras, speakers, stage props, dancers stretching, and a string quarter warming up and tuning. It was impressive. With a furrowed brow, the man mumbled a short but profound question under his breath: "Where's Jesus?"

Amidst the chaos of the holidays, a sad irony occurs: we often forget where Christ is and what role he possesses. He is not a guest speaker at church. He is not on the advisory board at church. He is not a mere idea that the church uses to market itself. He is not subservient to the whims and fashions in the church. He is not an angel who ministers to the church. The risen Lord Jesus Christ is the supreme head of his church. He is the undisputed ruler of his church. He is the sinless Bridegroom of his church. He is the supreme governor of his church.

In his letter to the Corinthians, Paul likens the church to a body: "For just as the body is one and has many members [parts], and all the members of the body, though many, are one body, so it is with Christ" (1 Cor. 12:12). Drawing on this analogy, Paul elsewhere refers to Christ as the *head* of that body: "And he is the head of the body, the church. He is the beginning, the firstborn from the dead, that in everything he might be preeminent" (Col. 1:18). Unlike the head of a board of directors, Christ is the head of a living organism of called-out, redeemed, regenerate people called the church. Just as the head gives direction and life to our earthly bodies, Jesus Christ gives direction, life, vitality, power, and sustenance to his church through his Word and Spirit. Therefore, Paul refers to him as the "beginning" (Col. 1:18). The Greek word *arche* refers to primacy and superiority. He is the founder, initiator, and author of the church. Being called "the firstborn from the dead" (v. 18) does not refer to Jesus being the first of all created beings. Rather, it refers to highest rank.

Paul's final description of the risen Christ is instructive: "that in everything he might be preeminent" (v. 18). Make no mistake, Christ *is* preeminent. We do not crown him as Lord, he simply *is* Lord. John's greetings to the various churches in his Revelation affirms Christ's ascended status: "Grace to you and peace from him who is and who was and who is to come, and from the seven spirits who are before his throne, and from Jesus Christ the faithful witness, the firstborn of the dead, and the ruler of the kings on earth" (Rev. 1:4-5).

O, that someone would sit next to the man who asked, "Where's Jesus?" and tell him these things! As precious souls gather for Christmas services this year, may they be awestruck with the preeminence and majesty of the church's head, Jesus Christ! May we speak, sing, and preach in such a way as to answer the question readily and solidly, "Where's Jesus?"

THE INTERCEDING ADVOCATE

Who is to condemn? Christ Jesus is the one who died—more than that, who was raised—who is at the right hand of God, who indeed is interceding for us.

(Romans 8:34)

One of the best gifts I ever received as a young man was a yellow single-string bow and a handful of arrows with sharp tips. My imagination would run wild as I stalked through the yard looking for bad guys insidiously disguised as trees, bushes, pinecones. If our neighborhood had any idea of how many thugs, robbers, and super villains I vanquished with that bow, they would have hosted a parade in my honor. On one muggy afternoon, I drew down on a large menace in the backyard (disguised as a mature Florida pine tree, of course). I had him in my sights as I pulled the arrow back to my right cheek, lined up the shot, and let it fly. It glanced off the target on the right side and flew right into the door of my dad's truck. Dumbfounded, I stared at the dent and scratch on the driver's side of that black Chevy for what seemed an eternity. I knew I was in trouble. I needed someone to speak for me; I could barely breathe. I needed a hero to take up my pathetic cause. In short, I needed someone to intercede on my behalf.

Many people refer to Matthew 6:5-15 as *The Lord's Prayer*. However, I would argue that John 17 is more appropriately called by this grand title. The reason is simple: Matthew 6 instructs us how to pray; John 17 shows us how the Lord prayed. Also called his *High Priestly Prayer*, John's gospel gives us an intimate glimpse into the intercessory activity of Jesus on behalf of his people: "I am praying for them, I am not praying for the world but for those whom you have given me, for they are yours . . . I do not ask for these only, but also for those who will believe in me through their word" (Jn. 17:9, 20). In this beautiful prayer, the Lord Jesus *intercedes* for his people—a word that caries the idea of bringing a petition before a king.

Scripture affirms the intercessory role of Christ and his exclusive prerogative to be the only One who can effectively do so: "For there is one God, and there is one mediator [intercessor] between God and men, the man Christ Jesus" (1 Tim. 2:5). Just as the numerous earthly priests served as mediators between the sinful people of Israel and Yahweh, Jesus Christ is the perfect, final, and eternal priest who can mediate on behalf of his people. The author of Hebrews makes a stark contrast between the quality of these priesthoods:

> The former priests were many in number, because they were prevented by death from continuing in office, but he [Christ] holds his priesthood permanently, because he continues forever. Consequently, he is able to save to the uttermost those who draw near to God through him, since he always lives to make intercession for them (Heb. 7:23-25).

Our King is also the priest whose sacrifice on the cross, resurrection to life, and ascension to glory secure his role as the perfect and permanent intercessor for his sinful people.

Having encouraged the Roman believers that Satan's accusations would not stick against them (Rom. 8:33), Paul goes on to ground his confidence in the Person and work of the risen, reigning Lord Jesus: "Who is to condemn? Christ Jesus is the one who died—more than that, who was raised—who is at the right hand of God, who indeed is interceding for us" (Rom. 8:34). My guilt in firing the arrow on that fateful day called for an intercessor to plead my case. More than that, my guilt before a holy God cries out for a meditator. Glory to our risen King, he ever lives to intercede for us! Although we may grow weary in the long days of winter, our Savior never tires as our advocate.

DECEMBER 23
THE KING OF ANGELS

[Jesus] has gone into heaven and is at the right hand of God, with angels, authorities, and powers having been subjected to him.

(1 Peter 3:22)

Unlike any other time of year, the holiday season brings with it a dramatic spike in the public's interest with angels. From January through November, one would be hard-pressed to hear a song mentioning angels playing in a department store or mall. In December, however, angels seem to be all the rage. Granted, there are songs from the fifties that liken a favorite gal to an angel but this not the issue at hand. Around Christmas, our relatively irreligious, post-Christian culture somehow makes room for the prominence of angels. Mere sentimentality? Perhaps. Nevertheless, it is still interesting to see this shift take place. The intrigue is heightened when one sees angels atop Christmas trees, angels on holiday greeting cards, and angels as lawn ornaments yet images or honorable mentions of the risen, ascended, sovereign Christ are scant at best. Are angels more to be honored than Jesus? Is he merely an exalted angel himself? Should someone have a robust theology of angels with an anemic theology of Christ? What is his relationship to these spiritual beings?

To be fair, angels are mentioned numerous times in Scripture. Most notably, they play a prominent role in the events surrounding the birth of Christ: "In the sixth month the angel Gabriel was sent from God to a city of Galilee named Nazareth, to a virgin betrothed to a man whose name was Joseph, of the house of David. And the virgin's name was Mary" (Lk. 1:26-27). Another well-known scene included the activity of angels (much to the surprise of some unsuspecting shepherds): "And suddenly there was with the angel a multitude of the heavenly host praising God and saying, 'Glory to God in the highest, and on earth peace among those with whom he is pleased!'" (Lk. 2:13-14). Although present and active in Scripture, are angels superior to Jesus?

It is often instructive to learn from someone else's mistakes. In the case of the apostle John, we are poised to learn a great deal about the nature and position of angels:

> And the angel said to me, "Write this: Blessed are those who are invited to the marriage supper of the Lamb." And he said to me, "These are the true words of God." Then I fell down at his feet to worship him, but he said to me, "You must not do that! I am a fellow servant with you and your brothers who hold to the testimony of Jesus. Worship God" (Rev. 19:9-10).

Can you imagine John's embarrassment? He bows in reverence to a heavenly being only to be reprimanded and told to stand up immediately. Note the urgency in the angel's voice when he proclaims, "You must not do that!" It is as if the angel was himself embarrassed by John's overture of respect. The angel was teaching us about the true status of angels: beautiful, mighty, and loyal servants and messengers of God who are *not* to be worshiped as if they were God.

The apostle Peter tells us the position to which Christ ascended and is now reigning: "[He] has gone into heaven and is at the right hand of God, with angels, authorities, and powers having been subjected to him" (1 Pet. 3:22). Like John, blushing as he rises from the ground, we should realize that angels are to be appreciated but not revered, recognized but not worshiped. Jesus Christ is the only One worthy of worship and adoration. Not only is he the King of kings, he is the King of angels.

DECEMBER 24

THE OBJECT OF PRAISE

*And they sang a new song, saying, "Worthy are you to take the
scroll and to open its seals, for you were slain, and by your
blood you ransomed people for God from every tribe
and language and people and nation."*

(Revelation 5:9)

Many of us will gather with family tonight and tomorrow
for food, gifts, and laughter. If your family is like mine,
there may also be several little ones adding fuel to the
chaos of a packed kitchen or living room. The excitement and
anticipation of Christmas eve often throws boys and girls into
a frenzy of joy. Their sugar-induced state of ecstasy may also
lead to a proverbial contest between the children to see who
can claim the spotlight and garner the most attention from the
captive audience of adult onlookers. Cartwheels, heartfelt ballads,
favorite jokes, or displays of strength are all means of claiming
the coveted laughter and affirmation of parents, grandparents,
aunts, uncles, and cousins. How can I speak so confidently about
such things? I did the same things when I was young.

Let's leave our scene in the crowded house and go up—way
up into heaven. What or who is the object of attention there?
What captures the gaze and attention of deceased Christians,
angels, and heavenly beings? Scripture indeed affirms that all of
heaven is riveted upon one thing. Considering John's revelation,
the object of heavenly praise is:

A lion—John's revelation of the throne room of heaven reveals
what (or who) can open the seals of the title deed to the earth. The

one who possesses the authority and power to do so is described as a lion: "And one of the elders said to me, 'Weep no more; behold, the Lion of the tribe of Judah, the Root of David, has conquered, so that he can open the scroll and its seven seals" (Rev. 5:5). This verse hearkens all the way back to the book of Genesis where a prophecy was given concerning this Judah-lion:

> Judah is a lion's cub; from the prey, my son, you have gone up. He stooped down; he crouched as a lion and as a lioness; who dares rouse him? The scepter shall not depart from Judah, nor the rulers staff from between his feet, until tribute comes to him; and to him shall be the obedience of the peoples (Gen. 49:9-10).

The lion's cub in Genesis is now a fully-grown lion with a regal mane and a deep growl. He indeed has conquered his prey—Satan, death, and hell lay bloody and defeated at his regal paws.

A lamb—John's vision takes a paradoxical turn: "And between the throne and the four living creatures and among the elders I saw a Lamb standing, as though it had been slain, with seven horns and with seven eyes" (Rev. 5:6). The lion who conquered did so as a little lamb, a lamb who appeared to John as bloody but living. Although wounded, he had seven horns—a sign of perfect power and authority. Clearly, this is no ordinary lamb.

When this lion-lamb approaches the throne, and takes the scroll as a sign of his possessing sovereign authority over all the earth, the entire court of heaven erupts in praise: "And when he had taken the scroll, the four living creatures and the twenty-four elders fell down before the Lamb, each holding a harp, and golden bowls full of incense, which are the prayers of the saints" (Rev. 5:8). King Jesus is the lion-lamb of heaven. At this moment, he is receiving exuberant praise and worship, a tidal wave of joy that will envelope all his people for a billion eternities to come.

DECEMBER 25
BEHOLD, HE COMES!

*Then I saw heaven opened, and behold, a white horse!
The one sitting on it is called Faithful and True, and
in righteousness he judges and makes war.*

(Revelation 19:11)

Today we formally celebrate the birth of Christ. Classic songs such as *Silent Night* and *Away in a Manger* draw our minds and hearts to the blessed day when the God-man came into the world to secure the salvation of his people. This is well and good. However, the plan of redemption did not end with a gentle babe in a manger (though I am positive Jesus cried like all other babies). Although he came into this world weak, helpless, and small, his return will be nothing of the sort. On this Christmas Day, amidst both laughter and sorrow, let us turn our attention away from the babe of Bethlehem and look to Revelation 19:11-16 as we ponder the return of the King:

A White Horse—The point in John's vision is not so much that Jesus will literally stride through the atmosphere on a literal white horse. The main point concerns what the horse represents. In his first coming, Jesus rode a colt as a sign of servanthood (Zech. 9:9). At his second coming, he will ride a war horse as a conquering general. All his enemies will be destroyed because "in righteousness he judges and makes war" (v. 11).

Eyes like fire and a crown of jewels—No one, great or small, will be able to escape the scrutiny of his holy judgments. His eyes pierce to the very souls of men: "And no creature is hidden from his sight, but all are naked and exposed to the eyes of him to whom we must give an account" (Heb. 4:13). Does he have the right to pass judgment? The brow that once bled from a crown of thorns now wears a jewel-laden crown—a silent declaration that his King alone has the right and ability to render holy judgment.

He wears a robe dipped in blood—Make no mistake, this is not *his* blood. His robe is spattered with the blood of his enemies. Satan, sin, and death have all suffered mortal wounds from the rider on the white horse: "He disarmed the rulers and authorities and put them to open shame, by triumphing over them in [the cross]" (Col. 2:15). In his death, resurrection, and ascension, Jesus Christ has defeated his enemies and achieved a perfect and complete salvation for his people.

His people rejoice in his domination—The "armies of heaven" (v. 14) are with him but they are not carrying weapons as if Christ needs help. When he returns to subdue his enemies permanently, he will dominate singlehandedly. More precisely, his word will suffice to slay his enemies. His ability to conquer all remaining rebellion, human or angelic, at his return is supported by the fact that he will "rule them with a rod of iron." His judgments will be uncontested as he treads "the winepress of the fury of the wrath of God the Almighty."

This may seem like a somber note to strike on Christmas Day. However, it should be cause for great rejoicing. Wickedness, evil, and rebellion will be dealt with and God's people will be vindicated. Moreover, if you are reading this and yet are not bowing to Jesus Christ, there is still time to repent. This Christmas we rejoice in the King whose mission cannot fail. We long for the return of the "King of kings and Lord of lords." Come, Lord Jesus!